QUEENS OF THE ANIMAL UNIVERSE

RING-TAILED LEMUR PRINCESSES

Rulers of the Troop

by Jaclyn Jaycox

PEBBLE
a capstone imprint

Published by Pebble, an imprint of Capstone
1710 Roe Crest Drive,
North Mankato, Minnesota 56003
capstonepub.com

Library of Congress Cataloging-in-Publication Data
Names: Jaycox, Jaclyn, 1983- author.
Title: Ring-tailed lemur princesses : rulers of the troop / by Jaclyn Jaycox.
Description: North Mankato, Minnesota : Pebble, [2023] | Series: Queens of the animal universe | Includes bibliographical references and index. | Audience: Ages 5-8 | Audience: Grades K-1 | Summary: "Screech! A female ring-tailed lemur screams loudly. It is a warning for an intruder to stay away. Females lead ring-tailed lemur troops. They hunt, defend their territories, and care for young. Take a close look at ring-tailed lemurs and the important roles princesses play to ensure a troop's survival"-- Provided by publisher.
Identifiers: LCCN 2021054278 (print) | LCCN 2021054279 (ebook) | ISBN 9781666343069 (hardcover) | ISBN 9781666343120 (paperback) | ISBN 9781666343182 (pdf) | ISBN 9781666343304 (kindle edition)
Subjects: LCSH: Ring-tailed lemur--Behavior--Juvenile literature. | Social hierarchy in animals--Juvenile literature. | Social behavior in animals--Juvenile literature. | Animal societies--Juvenile literature.
Classification: LCC QL737.P95 J395 2023 (print) | LCC QL737.P95 (ebook) |DDC 599.8/315--dc23/eng/20211122
LC record available at https://lccn.loc.gov/2021054278
LC ebook record available at https://lccn.loc.gov/2021054279

Editor: Carrie Sheely; Designer: Bobbie Nuytten; Media Researcher: Morgan Walters; Production Specialist: Polly Fisher

Image Credits
Alamy: Michele Burgess, 23; Capstone Press, 7; Getty Images: Darrell Gulin, 5, Floridapfe from S.Korea Kim in cherl, 28; Shutterstock: Azahara Perez, 9, BlackFarm, 14, BrightRainbow, (dots background) design element, coxy58, 27, David Havel, 29, Eric Gevaert, 13, GUDKOV ANDREY, 6, Irena Kofman, 21, Jez Bennett, 8, KAMONRAT, 11, MattiaATH, 17, MyImages - Micha, 25, Ondrej_Novotny_92, 15, Piotr Krzeslak, Cover, Sean McGrae, 19, WinWin artlab, (crowns) design element

All internet sites appearing in back matter were available and accurate when this book was sent to press.

Printed and bound in the USA. 4882

Table of Contents

Words in **bold** are in the glossary.

Lemur Princesses Rule!

In the animal world, males are often the leaders. They are usually bigger and stronger than females. But some animals break the rules. When it comes to ring-tailed lemurs, the females take charge!

Female lemurs are known as princesses. A princess is the head of her family. Let's learn more about these amazing animal rulers!

A ring-tailed lemur family is made up of mainly females, who are the group's leaders.

Meet the Ring-Tailed Lemur

What do a lemur, gorilla, and human have in common? They are all **primates**! Primates are a kind of **mammal**. Mammals have hair. Young mammals drink milk from their mothers.

A ring-tailed lemur stands to look around on Madagascar.

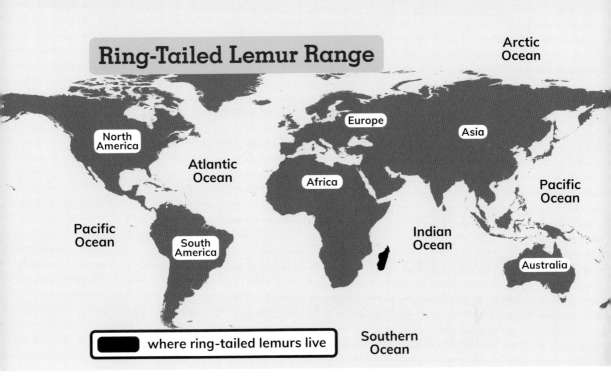

Ring-Tailed Lemur Range

Arctic Ocean

Europe

Asia

North America

Atlantic Ocean

Africa

Pacific Ocean

Pacific Ocean

South America

Indian Ocean

Australia

where ring-tailed lemurs live

Southern Ocean

There are more than 100 kinds of lemurs. Lemurs are only found near Africa. Ring-tailed lemurs live on Madagascar.

Lemurs are the most **endangered** mammals in the world. Almost all kinds are in danger of dying out. Only between 2,000 and 2,500 ring-tailed lemurs are left in the wild.

Look up! What is jumping through the trees? It's a ring-tailed lemur! These lemurs live in different **habitats**. Some live in forests. Others live in hot, dry areas. They spend about half of their time on the ground. The rest of the time they are high in trees.

Ring-tailed lemurs can jump a distance of about 25 feet (7.6 meters).

Eating fruit helps ring-tailed lemurs get the water they need.

Lemurs eat **insects** and fruit. They eat leaves, bark, and flowers too. Lemurs don't often drink water. They get most of their water from food.

Lemur Bodies

Ring-tailed lemurs are named for their tails. Their tails have black and white rings. Their tails are longer than their bodies. The lemurs' tails can grow up to 2 feet (0.6 meters) long.

Ring-tailed lemurs are about the size of house cats. They weigh about 6 pounds (2.7 kilograms). In many primates, males are bigger than females. But not ring-tailed lemurs. They are all the same size. It's very hard to tell them apart.

Ring-tailed lemurs usually have 12 or 13 tail rings of each color.

Ring-tailed lemurs have red-brown or gray fur on their backs. They have white stomachs and faces. Dark rings circle their eyes. Lemurs have pointy, black noses.

Lemurs have big bright yellow or amber eyes. They can see very well at night.

Lemurs also have an amazing sense of smell. It helps them find food. It helps them find their family members too.

Ring-tailed lemurs have large, round eyes.

Lemur Troops

Lemurs live in family groups. These groups are called troops. Troops can have up to 30 lemurs. Females stay in the same troop their whole lives. Males switch troops every few years.

Members of a lemur troop huddle together.

Whoop! Howl! Lemurs are noisy! They use their voices to **communicate** with one another. Ring-tailed lemurs communicate in other ways too. They raise their tails in the air. This helps the lemurs stay together. They use their scent to mark their **territory**. This tells other lemur families to stay away.

Some ring-tailed lemur sounds can be heard by people about 0.5 mile (0.8 kilometer) away.

Ladies First

A male lemur eats a tasty piece of fruit. A female lemur eyes his snack. She thinks it looks good too! She leaps over to him. She grabs it away. Snatch! The male does not try to get it back. He heads off to look for more.

In a troop, one female is the leader. But all females **rank** higher than males. Females are the first to eat. Sometimes a male will eat out of turn. A female will take away his food.

Princesses get their choice
of food before the males.

Females have their pick of sleeping spots. A male might be snoozing in a good spot. A female will push him out of the way.

Females also get their pick of sunbathing spots. To sunbathe, lemurs sit while holding their front legs up. The sun warms their bellies.

A lemur sunbathes.

Mothers usually give birth to one baby. The baby stays with its mother. It holds on to her stomach for the first two weeks. Then the baby rides on its mother's back.

After a few months, the young begin to let go. They walk and climb on their own. But if there's danger, they jump back on their mother's back. Female lemurs protect their young.

A baby lemur clings
to its mother's back.

Female ring-tailed lemurs find new territories. They choose areas with plenty of food for their troop. Having a good food source helps the troop survive.

Both male and female lemurs mark the territory. But females are in charge of protecting it. They fiercely defend their territory. Sometimes other lemurs get too close. The females fight them off. They often do this with babies on their backs!

A ring-tailed lemur marks its scent on a tree.

Working Together

Female ring-tailed lemurs have hard jobs. Males don't help raise young. In fights over territory, the males stand back. They let the females battle it out. Females tell the troop when and where to move. But they don't have to do everything alone. Female lemurs help one another.

All females in a troop help raise the young. They usually give birth around the same time. They help feed one another's babies. They get into groups so the young can play together.

A princess cares for two babies
while another lemur rests.

Female ring-tailed lemurs have a strong bond. One way they bond is by **grooming**. They have special teeth for this. The teeth act like a comb. Females spend a lot of time grooming one another.

Scientists have questions about ring-tailed lemurs. For many animals, either the males or females are larger. The bigger of the two is usually the leader. But all ring-tailed lemurs are very much alike. Scientists continue to learn more about them. But one thing is for sure—female lemurs are up to the job of ruling the troop!

A ring-tailed lemur grooms another troop member.

Amazing Lemur Facts

In a fight between a male and female lemur, the female always wins.

Male ring-tailed lemurs have "stink fights" to fight over the females. They rub their tails over their scent glands and wave them around. The stinkiest one wins!

Lemurs are important seed spreaders. They eat fruit with seeds. When they poop, they spread the seeds to new places. New plants can grow from them.

Ring-tailed lemurs can meow and purr like cats.

Ring-tailed lemurs are most active in the early morning and late afternoon.

Scientists believe lemurs lived in Africa millions of years ago. They may have floated to Madagascar on logs.

Ring-tailed lemurs live about 16 years in the wild.

In Latin, the word lemur means "ghost." When seeing the animals for the first time, scientists thought they looked like ghosts.

Glossary

communicate (kuh-MYOO-nuh-kate)—to share information

endangered (in-DAYN-juhrd)—in danger of dying out

groom (GROOM)—to keep clean

habitat (HAB-uh-tat)—the natural place and conditions in which an animal or plant lives

insect (in-SEKT)—a small animal with a hard outer shell, six legs, three body sections, and two antennae; most insects have wings

mammal (MAM-uhl)—a warm–blooded animal that breathes air; mammals have hair or fur; female mammals feed milk to their young

primate (PRYE-mate)—a member of the group of intelligent animals that includes humans, apes, and monkeys

rank (RANGK)—to take or have a position in relation to others in a group

territory (TER-uh-tor-ee)—the land on which an animal grazes or hunts for food and raises its young

Read More

Bodden, Valerie. *Lemurs*. Mankato, MN: Creative Education, 2019.

Jaycox, Jaclyn. *Lemurs*. North Mankato, MN: Capstone, 2021.

Storm, Marysa. *Ring-Tailed Lemurs*. Mankato, MN: Black Rabbit Books, 2020.

Internet Sites

Animal Fact Guide: Ring-Tailed Lemur
animalfactguide.com/animal-facts/ring-tailed-lemur/

National Geographic Kids: Ring-Tailed Lemur
kids.nationalgeographic.com/animals/mammals/facts/ring-tailed-lemur

San Diego Zoo Wildlife Alliance: Lemur
animals.sandiegozoo.org/animals/lemur

Index

Author Biography

Behind the Lens Photography

Jaclyn Jaycox is a children's book author and editor. When she's not writing, she loves reading and spending time with her family. She lives in southern Minnesota with her husband, two kids, and a spunky goldendoodle.